Minc

The Most Effective Techniques
Connect With Your Inner Self to Reach Your Goals Easily and Peacefully

Positive Psychology Coaching Series

Copyright © 2017 by Ian Tuhovsky

Author's blog: www.mindfulnessforsuccess.com
Author's Amazon profile: amazon.com/author/iantuhovsky
Instagram profile: https://instagram.com/mindfulnessforsuccess

Please be aware that every e-book and "short read" I publish is written truly by me, with thoroughly researched content 100% of the time. Unfortunately, there's a huge number of low quality, cheaply outsourced spam titles on the Kindle non-fiction market these days, created by various internet marketing companies. **I don't tolerate these books. I want to provide you with high quality, so if you think that one of my books/short reads can be improved in any way, please contact me at:**

contact@mindfulnessforsuccess.com

I will be very happy to hear from you, because that's who I write my books for!

Introduction

What's the difference between successful people and unsuccessful ones? Unless we're talking about athletes, the answer is their minds. Successful people have more of *something*—more courage, maybe, or more persistence, more inspiration—and that something is certain qualities of mind.

But what is mind, exactly? We should stop and ask this question, because the mind is in so many ways very transparent to us. It is the window through which we experience everything—ourselves and our world - but we rarely stop to consider the window itself. What is it made of? What is its nature?

These questions may sound too philosophical, but, in fact, **they're very practical**. They are questions about the dirt and soil, the nitty gritty of life. Your mind shapes your action in the world, **which in turn defines the contour and direction of your life**. If you want to change your life and find success, you'll have to work with your mind. You'll have to work with its emotions, doubts, hopes, fears, deceptions, inertia, and energy. So it's worthwhile to get familiar with your mind and useful to make friends with it.

The mind is something like a reservoir of thoughts, feelings, perceptions, and intentions powered by emotional energy. That energy **can either be caught up pointlessly in bad habits and hangups,** or it **can be harnessed in the pursuit of your goals and propel you to success**. It goes without saying that successful people got that way by doing the latter. Among the defining characteristics of successful people are the following powerful mental attitudes:

- **They adapt to and embrace change.** Successful people don't just let changing circumstances come and kick them in the butt. They don't bury their heads in the sand and refuse to adapt to the turning of the tide. Instead, they understand the shifting, impermanent nature of things and meet changes with an inner attitude of acceptance and a willingness to learn and adapt.

- **They grab the reins of destiny.** Successful people do not feel resentful about the past. They don't blame their parents, bosses, coworkers, ex-lovers—whoever—for their problems. Instead, they accept what has happened in the past as over and done with and look to the future. Without waiting for a lucky break to come along, they take charge of their own lives and shape them according to their desires.

- **They have an attitude of curiosity.** Successful

people are interested in new things and new ideas. Their approach to the world is that it is a big, fascinating place that has many lessons to learn. They understand a key truth of human existence: the realm of things we *don't* know is infinitely bigger than the realm of things we *do* know. They stand with one foot in the known realm and the other in the unknown and always keep their eyes open.

- **They understand interdependence.** Successful people know they don't accomplish anything alone. Everything you do, whether you receive direct help or not, depends on the efforts of others. Successful people understand this and have a sense of gratitude to others. Because they cultivate good relationships with others, they always find assistance when they need it.

- **They have persistence and a courageous spirit.** Successful people don't let defeats, setbacks, and disadvantages keep them from pursuing their goals. They are "happy warriors" who, instead of getting discouraged, push past obstacles with vision, focus, and the outrageous determination of conquerors.

In this book, I want to introduce you to mindfulness techniques that will help you cultivate these and other qualities of mind that will bring you not only success, but greater happiness, contentment, and inner resourcefulness for dealing with the many challenges and opportunities of life.

Your Free Mindfulness E-book

I really appreciate the fact that you took an interest in my work! I also think it's great you are into self-development and proactively making your life better.

This is why I would love to offer you a free, complimentary 120-page e-book.

It's also about mindfulness, but more precisely, about Mindfulness-Based Stress and Anxiety Management Techniques.

It will provide you with a solid foundation to kick-start your self-development success and help you become much more relaxed, but at the same time, more focused and effective person. All explained in plain English, and it's a useful free supplement to this book.

To download your e-book, please visit:

http://www.tinyurl.com/mindfulnessgift

Enjoy!
Thanks again for being my reader! It means a lot to me!

Chapter 1. Mindfulness

Jon Kabat-Zinn, a leading pioneer of the mindfulness movement and the founder of Mindfulness-Based Stress Reduction (MBSR), defines mindfulness as "paying attention on purpose, in the present moment, nonjudgmentally." Let's take a look at this definition more closely.

- "Paying attention..." At any given moment, the mind has its attention on something or another. But there are different qualities of attention. Sometimes attention is focused and steady, sometimes scattered and unstable. Mindfulness belongs to the focused and steady kind of attention.

- "On purpose..." Specifically, mindfulness is *purposeful* attention. If you're mindful of something—the breath, let's say—it's because you purposefully directed your attention there. So we're not talking about random, scattered attention. We're talking about focused, intentionally directed attention.

- "In the present moment..." There is no other moment in which to do anything. Mindfulness does not indulge in memories of yesterday or hang on to happy nostalgia or bad feelings from the past. Mindfulness does not get entangled in hopes and fears about the future. Mindfulness is about cultivating an awareness and appreciation of the here and now, of the richness of your present experience.

- "Nonjudgmentally." Especially in meditation, mindfulness is not about accepting or rejecting anything. Whatever thoughts, feelings, or perceptions come up in the context of mindfulness are not regarded as good or bad, but as simply part of the colorful tapestry of mind.

Why Mindfulness?

Recent scientific research into ancient meditation techniques has demonstrated the numerous benefits of mindfulness for body and mind. In particular, mindfulness decreases stress, anxiety, depression, irritability, emotional reactivity, and fatigue. It also reduces what psychologists call "rumination"— that is, compulsive thinking with negative affect. It regulates emotions and improves concentration, working memory, and cognitive flexibility. It even increases relationship satisfaction.[1]

---

1   Barnes et al., "What Are the Benefits of Mindfulness? A Practice Review of Psychotherapy-Related Research," *Psychotherapy* 48 (2011), 198-208.

Here are some of the other empirically supported benefits of mindfulness:

- Office workers who practiced stress reduction techniques based on mindfulness for twenty minutes each and every day testified to an average eleven-percent decrease in perceived stress.[2]
- Eight weeks of MBSR techniques bring about development in the immune profile systems of individuals with prostate or breast cancer, corresponding to a reduction in the symptoms of depression.[3]
- A combination of patients suffering from cancer who tried Mindfulness-Based Stress Reduction techniques exhibited substantial improvement in their overall mood with decreased levels of stress.[4]
- Mindfulness-Based Cognitive Therapy, a branch of MBSR, reduced the probability of repetition for patients

---

2 Maryanna Klatt, Assistant Professor of Clinical Allied Medicine, Janet Buckworth of the College of Education and Human Ecology and William Malarkey of the College of Medicine, Ohio State Pilot Study: Workplace Yoga And Meditation Can Lower Feelings Of Stress http://researchnews.osu.edu/archive/mindful.htm

3 Carlson et al, "Mindfulness- Based Stress Reduction in Relation to Quality of Life, Mood, Symptoms of Stress, and Immune Parameters in Breast and Prostate Cancer Outpatients," *Psychosomatic Medicine: Journal Of Biobehavioral Medicine*, 65.4 (2003), 571–581.

4 Speca et al., "A Randomized, Wait-List Controlled Clinical Trial: The Effect of a Mindfulness Meditation-Based Stress Reduction Program on Mood and Symptoms of Stress in Cancer Outpatients," *Psychosomatic Medicine* 62.5 (2000), 613-622.

who had experienced at least three bouts of depression.[5]

- After fifteen weeks of practicing MBSR techniques, students under counseling reported enhanced emotional and physical well-being, with a positive influence on their therapeutic relationships and psychotherapy skills.[6]

Mindfulness and Meditation

The centerpiece of the practice of mindfulness is meditation. I think we need to explain what meditation is all about, because even though "mindfulness" has become a popular buzzword, the subject of psychological research and many a TED talk, some misconceptions and doubts still persist around the word "meditation."

Meditation is not some new agey preoccupation. It does not require you to chant in some weird language or wear exotic clothes. In fact, you don't need to pick up a new set of beliefs or buy into a new religion to do meditation. All you need is the willingness to sit on your own butt and spend a little time

5   Baer, R. A., "Mindfulness training as a clinical intervention: A conceptual and empirical review." *Clinical Psychology: Science and Practice*, 10 (2003), 125–143.
6   Schure et al., "Mind–Body Medicine and the Art of Self-Care: Teaching Mindfulness to Counseling Students Through Yoga, Meditation, and Qigong," *Journal of Counseling & Development* 86.1 (2008), 47–56.

getting to know your mind.

You know which mind I'm talking about. I mean the mind that accompanies you everywhere you go. I mean your own thoughts, feelings, emotions, memories, doubts, interests, hangups, and confusions. I mean your own moments of clarity, your own attention and intelligence. These very ordinary aspects of your mind don't have anything to do with metaphysical belief systems. They are simply the interior part of your lived experience. Meditation is the practice of getting more familiar with them, of deepening your understanding of how your mind works and how its different moving parts condition your experience of the world—for better or for worse.

To do that, to gain this understanding, you need to spend some time refining your attention so that it can rest for a length of time on some object without distraction. In other words, you need to cultivate mindfulness. The object of meditation could be anything, but most commonly, one focuses on mindfulness of the breath. But before we get into that, I want to address some of the most common objections of people who are reluctant to start meditation.

Common Objections to Meditation

If you're like most people who haven't already made meditation a part of their lives, it might be a bit intimidating for you. There are a number of excuses people have for shying away from getting into meditation, but they all boil down to just being reluctant to begin something unfamiliar.

Remember what we said earlier about how successful people have curiosity and courage? Both of them come into play when we're learning to do something for the first time, and meditation is no exception. So let's take a look at these excuses one by one and see if they really stack up.

- **It sounds boring.** Well, it is boring—sometimes. But so is just about anything else you will do on the road to success. A good analogy is learning to play guitar. There's a lot of boredom in the process. Learning scales? Let's be honest, it's not so exciting. But you have to do it if you want to get really good. And the payoff is that you'll improve your chops and be able to pull off some awesome licks. It's the same with meditation. If you want the payoff, you have to go through some boredom.

  But let's think about boredom for a minute. We seldom ever take the chance to really experience boredom fully.

15

Usually we find it so irritating that we become restless and start looking for any occupation or distraction to relieve ourselves. Or we ignore the boredom and plug into whatever work we're doing.

Meditation doesn't offer much escape from boredom, actually. Instead, we're just left with the only option of sitting with boredom and feeling boredom's energy. Then, when we feel it properly, the restless energy of boredom starts to relax. It turns out that restlessness is precisely what we find so irritating about boredom in the first place. So as it relaxes, we relax and we ease into a natural boredom, if we can even call it that. Then we don't feel compelled to find some preoccupation to relieve ourselves. And that can be a very refreshing experience.

- **Meditation is too religious/spiritual/woo-woo for me.** You don't have to be "spiritual" or "religious" to get into meditation. Meditation isn't about the afterlife, the godhead, a higher power, or a more spiritual plane of being. It's about the here and now and the solid ground you're sitting on. It's about getting to know yourself and your own mind. It's very realistic—almost too realistic, because it takes away any notions you might have of escape from the present situation. So, far from being all about a spiritual journey and so on, meditation doesn't leave you any fantasies or metaphysical notions to lean on.

- **I don't have the time.** We all have busy lives and everyone's pressed for time these days. But I bet you could spare just ten minutes a day for something that's scientifically proven to reduce stress and enhance your cognitive abilities. And that improved sense of mental wellbeing will improve your performance in other areas of life. With a more relaxed, healthy, and attentive mind, you'll actually save time by completing tasks with greater focus and efficiency.

- **My mind is too busy to meditate.** That's not a problem. In fact, don't you think that sounds like a very good reason to meditate? You don't have to force your mind to relax or be some kind of superstar meditator. It's not about playing whack-a-mole with your thoughts and trying to silence your inner dialogue. Thoughts are not your enemy in meditation; they are just part of the energy of the mind. Just sit down with yourself, and your mind will naturally come to rest on its own without any interference on your part. And you will find out what a joy that can be.

- **I can't sit still.** It's natural to fidget a bit. And, to tell you a secret, after more than ten years of meditating, I still find myself doing it sometimes. Does that make you feel better? But if sitting cross-legged doesn't work for you, you can find another position. You can sit in a chair or on a couch. You can even lie down, if you can manage not to fall asleep in that position.

- **I don't want to be alone with my mind.** Ah, at last we come to the truth. Most of the excuses not to meditate boil down to this: it just freaks us out to sit alone with our minds, without any option for escapism and distractions. **By avoiding meditation, we avoid ourselves.**

  But we can't really avoid ourselves, can we? **Whether we meditate or not, we have to live with ourselves in any case**. Given that we don't have any choice about that, we might as well get to know ourselves and make friends with ourselves. And I promise you it's not as scary as you think.

Finally, let's consider one last excuse commonly given by people reluctant to try meditation:

- **I don't know how to meditate.** No one knows how to do anything before they try it—except for simple physical activities like sitting and breathing. **As it turns out, these are the only two skills you need to start meditating right now**, so you don't have to worry about what you don't know. Just start with the basic practice, and the rest will come in time.

Once you get to the cushion, you'll find there really never was anything to worry about. You can approach meditation with the attitude of a scientist or an explorer. Come to meditation with an attitude of curiosity and openness, and you'll find that it's a richly rewarding experience.

Getting Into a Meditation Practice

Still, I realize it might be a little intimidating for you to just plop down on a cushion and start meditating right away. Maybe it's just that you feel kind of weird about it. So before we jump into the main practice, it might be a bit less daunting to take some baby steps and get used to the whole idea.

- **Walk and notice.** One easy way to get into the mindfulness thing is just to take a short walk around your neighborhood and try to notice things you've never seen before. In our busy lives, we're usually much too focused on where we're going, what we have to do today, or what happened yesterday to pay attention to our surroundings. So this exercise is all about reversing that trend and paying attention on purpose. Look for things you never noticed before—a sign you never saw, or a particular tree, or the color of a neighbor's house, a bicycle, whatever. I guarantee there will be no shortage of such things, and you might be quite surprised by some of them.

- **Stop and listen.** Wherever you are, just stop what you're doing and listen to whatever sounds you can hear. Maybe you hear the hum of some machinery in the background. Or the sounds of someone's conversation. A pencil sharpener grinding. Birds chirping. Someone laughing. A baby crying. Cars passing by.

These noises normally escape our notice, so the point of the exercise is to become more aware of the sounds that we usually just ignore. This is purposeful attention to your surroundings. Start right now. Before you even read the next sentence of this book, take three minutes, close your eyes, and just listen.

- **Check your emotional state.** At any point in time

during the day, you can stop what you're doing and check how things are going inside your head and heart. How do you feel right now? What kinds of emotions are occurring? Happiness, anger, sadness, irritation, amusement, love, desire? Get specific. Don't just think "anger," but try to identify if it's indignation you're feeling, or maybe rage, or bitterness. The ability to be precise about your emotions is called emotional granularity, and it's a good skill to have, because it helps with regulating your emotions.

Whatever you're feeling, try to regard it nonjudgmentally. Don't get caught up in judging it as good or bad. Think of your emotional state as like the weather. You're just checking to see what it's like out there. Is it calm or stormy? Rainy? Windy? Cloudy? Sunny? Hot or cold? Whatever the weather is like, it is constantly changing. Likewise, your current emotional state will give way to another one.

- **Pay attention to small things.** While you're out in nature, or at pretty much any other time when the opportunity comes along, you can pick up something small and observe it with close attention. It can be a rock, a blade of grass, a flower, a handful of soil—choose whatever. Look at it closely. Notice all its colors and shapes, the texture of its surface. Smell it. Run your fingers along its surface. Is it rough or smooth? Moist or dry? Maybe it's hard, soft, waxy, or brittle. You can examine it with all five senses (except maybe taste, depending on the object). Whatever it is, allow yourself to be curious about it, to observe and feel its qualities properly. This is also mindfulness.

How do you feel when you're observing things mindfully? Do you feel relaxed? Happy? Interested? Bored? Disgusted? (It doesn't have to be positive. Just be honest about it.) You can also pay attention to how your mind reacts to whatever you're observing—another kind of mindfulness.

- **Listen to music.** And I mean just listen to music. Put on a nice pair of headphones, sit down in a comfortable chair, and play some tracks you've never heard before. Don't occupy yourself with anything else, like work or checking emails or clipping your fingernails. Just listen very closely to the sounds. Don't pay much attention to the lyrics, the genre, and so on. Don't get too caught up in whether you like it or not. The idea is just to experience the music fully as a pure instance of sound, without judgment.

- **Enjoy your favorite drink.** Since this is a self-help book, I have to include a warning not to overindulge. So don't do that. My point is not to encourage any kind of dependency, but if you're the kind of person who likes a fine wine or Scotch, then that's the perfect opportunity to practice mindfulness. You can do the same with a cup of fine tea or coffee, or maybe a glass of freshly squeezed juice. Breathe the nose in deeply and really smell it properly. Take a sip and hold it in your mouth for a few seconds, allowing yourself to fully experience the taste and notice the subtleties of the flavor. Close your eyes if it helps.

  If you're a connoisseur, this is nothing new to you. What might be new is to learn that you've been practicing mindfulness and you didn't even know it.

- **Do some yoga.** Yoga is more approachable than meditation in some ways, because it's well-defined and physical. It's also pretty easy to find yoga classes everywhere these days. If you're looking for top-quality instruction, you might want to open your wallet. But to get started, you can probably find free yoga classes in your area without difficulty.

  Yoga is a lot more physically involved than meditation,

but it's still very relaxing and mindful. It also has a great number of health benefits, including reducing stress, removing excess fat, increasing flexibility and suppleness, and easing muscle and joint pain, to name just a few of the obvious ones.

You don't have to be super flexible to start, either. You just start with whatever positions you're able to do and take it from there. Yoga will help prepare you for meditation by making your mind more relaxed, releasing muscle tension, strengthening muscles in the back, and improving your posture and skeletal alignment.

Hey, if nothing else, it's also great way to meet people if you're single. So you might as well give it a try, you downward-facing dog, you.

- **Download an app.** Seriously. While it might feel pretty awkward to go sit on a cushion when you've never done anything like that before, if there's someone guiding you through the process, you won't be plagued by so many doubts about the whole thing. And there are many apps designed for just that. Use them. Should I name-drop one of them? Very well, try Headspace for starters. It makes meditation easy and has cute, amusing animations.

What all of these preliminaries have in common is that they all involve "paying attention, on purpose, in the present moment, nonjudgmentally." They are all pretty straightforward ways of getting into mindfulness that involve familiar activities. There's no limit to variations on this. You could practice this kind of mindfulness while cooking, for example, or washing the dishes. You could practice mindfulness while driving (in fact, I highly recommend it, as practicing mindlessness while driving could recklessly endanger your own and other's lives). But once you've got your feet wet, you will have a little experience of what mindfulness is all about. And pretty soon, if you want to make progress, you will probably want to get into a more formal and disciplined practice. So now we turn to the sitting practice of meditation.

How to Do Mindfulness Meditation

To get started practicing mindfulness, you don't need to make any huge commitments of your time. **Just taking five to ten minutes out of your day is enough to start reaping the benefits of mindfulness.** I like to think of my meditation sessions as time I take to stop and **be kind to myself**. Meditation gives me a chance to rest and get to know my own mind more deeply. It's a gesture of compassion, an **act of making friends with myself.**

Find a comfortable place to sit. It could be on a chair or a cushion on the floor. You can also lie down if you want, as long as you don't fall asleep. This is a good piece of advice I got from an experienced Thai Buddhist monk in one of many ancient temples in the city of Chiang Mai: to protect yourself from falling asleep and making sure you will be more alert, you might want to lie down on your side, while resting your head on your hand, like a statue of lying Buddha. This way, if you start falling asleep, your head will slip from your hand and you will immediately go back to alertness.

When sitting, the most important point is to keep your back straight but relaxed, as if your spine were a stack of coins. If the coins lean too far in any direction, they'll topple over. So try to keep your spine as vertical as possible, but without any strain.

Take a few moments to really feel the presence of your body where you are. Feel the weight of your body as you sit on the chair or cushion. Feel the pressure of your feet on the floor. This brings the body and mind together. It brings the mind into a present, sensory awareness of the body.

Draw a deep breath down into your stomach, then let it out like a big sigh. Pay attention to the sensations in your body. Do they feel good or bad? Are your muscles tensed or relaxed? You don't have to try to change anything, particularly; the point is just to be aware of any pleasant or unpleasant feelings.

The main part of the session is to turn your attention to the breath, so that your mind is filled with an awareness of the breath. As you breathe in, pay attention to the sensation of breathing, the way the inbreath feels in your nostrils, how the air fills your lungs as your chest and diaphragm expand. As you breathe out, your mind follows the breath, moving through your nose and dissolving into the space outside you.

To keep your mind from wandering from the breath, you may find it helpful to count. As you breathe in, count *one* in your head. As you breathe out, *two*. Count this way up to ten, then start again from *one*.

Don't worry if you become distracted. Distraction is a natural part of the practice. All sorts of thoughts and feelings will come up. Maybe you'll find yourself thinking about some work you have to do. Maybe, in your mind, you'll take a little vacation to Thailand or the Bahamas. Whatever the case, whatever arises in your mind is just *thinking*. It's neither good nor bad. Mentally label it *thinking*, without judging it, then gently return your mind to the breath, starting the count again from *one*.

As you mature in your practice, you might find that counting the breaths is just a little too much. You crave something a bit more subtle, a lighter touch. In that case, you can drop the counting and just pay attention to the sensation of the breath as it goes in and out, the rise and fall of your chest and diaphragm, whether the breath is long or short, deep or shallow, whether or not you pause between breaths. You'll soon find that the breath has many subtleties and variations.

Remember you don't need to alter anything about the breath. The point is not to try to change your breath or improve it in any way, but just to be with it. Let the breath fill your whole awareness. Let your mind get so absorbed in the breath it becomes one with it.

Again, after some time, it may seem that even paying attention to the in and out of the breath without counting is too overbearing a technique. Then you can try this: on the inbreath, rest your mind on the breath, become one with the breath. On the outbreath, completely relax your attention and don't focus on anything. As the outbreath dissolves into air outside you, let your attention also dissolve into space. On the inbreath, stay with the breath. On the outbreath, dissolve into openness.

This is a transition between mindfulness of the breath and

objectless meditation. In objectless meditation, you just rest your mind. You don't rest it anywhere, particularly, but you just let it be with the general space within and without you. You become one with that space. Your attention is on the totality of the present-moment environment as opposed to whatever is happening within it, so your mind becomes expansive and accommodating. In objectless meditation, you're not directing the attention anywhere, but you're also not distracted. Instead, you rest in a pervasive, precise awareness.

Finally, I want to say a word about consistency. If you really want to see the most positive results from the practice of mindfulness meditation, it is necessary to establish a daily practice and maintain it consistently. You don't have to sit for marathon sessions several hours long, as veteran meditators do. You can start seeing the benefits of mindfulness meditation, as I said above, with as few as five to ten minutes a day.

But the key to seeing results is *consistency*. Like any other skill, mindfulness must be worked on. And that will take daily practice. So if you feel that mindfulness meditation is a positive and worthwhile practice for you, if you are interested in getting to know your mind and making friends with yourself, fundamentally, then I urge you to make a daily habit of it.

Nonjudgmental Awareness and Working with Negative Thoughts

There really is no such thing as a bad meditation session. Whether you feel centered, calm, and fully mindful, or distracted, nervous, and antsy—or even dull or heavy—anything that comes up is fundamentally okay. Just the act of sitting and giving your time to the practice of mindfulness is a tremendously positive and sane thing to do.

With time, you'll find that this nonjudgmental attitude becomes more and more a part of you, a part of the way you relate to your thoughts and emotions. You'll develop a sense of space. Your mind, instead of feeling claustrophobic and cluttered, will feel open, relaxed, and spacious. When negative thoughts come up, there will be a sense of distance. You won't be gripped by negativity, nor will you feel a compulsion to reject it. Instead, you'll know how to allow negativity to just hang out in its own space, until it settles down all on its own.

Negativity takes many forms. Emotions, both positive and negative, first take place as a kind of motivating energy. This energy registers as a sensation somewhere in the body. Have you ever felt a sinking feeling in your gut when you encountered a major disappointment? Have you felt an expansive warmth in your heart or chest when you fell in love? How about when you get so furious that your "blood boils"—do you feel the heat literally rising through your body, a flush coming to your face? Scientific research confirms what common experience already tells us: emotions register as physical sensations in different parts of the body.[7]

On top of this raw emotional energy is a thick layer of conceptual thought. Thoughts tell a story about the emotions; they create an interpretation of what's going on in the mind. This narrative is like a constantly running director's commentary, which meditation traditions call "discursive thought" or "monkey mind." At this level, negativity becomes very problematic. Raw emotions are one thing, but the running commentary in our heads is complicated by self-deception, confirmation bias, and spin.

The practice of mindfulness allows us **to separate the felt energy of emotions and their physical components from the heavy layer of conceptual interpretation** that we add on top of them. This ability is what I like to call *emotional objectivity*. Developing this quality is key to using mindfulness to reduce stress, anxiety, depression, and negative thinking in general, and **allows you to retrain your mind to develop the positive mental habits that are the**

---

7   Nummenmaa et al. "Bodily Maps of Emotions." *Proceedings of the National Academy of Sciences* 111.2 (2014): 646–651.

hallmarks of a successful person.

Common Problems

Problems are part and parcel of the practice of mindfulness. There will never be a time when you're not encountering some kind of difficulty in your practice, because the whole point of the practice is to challenge you and make you grow. So if you find that your practice is going very smoothly with no problems at all, then something might be off.

But more likely you will run into all sorts of hiccups, irritations, and obstacles along the way. That's okay. It's just part of the process. Still, it's useful to know about some of the most commonly encountered problems in meditation and what to do about them.

- Pain in the body. If you sit for a long time in one position without moving, you might experience a bit of pain in your body, such as in your back or legs. You may even have a lot of pain. There are a few reasons why this might be.

  One is that you might not be sitting correctly. If you have pain in your back, for example, you can try adjusting.

Check your posture. Is it straight, or are you slumping? Are you actually leaning forward or back? It's okay to adjust your position if you find something wrong. As you progress in the practice, you might find that making small adjustments is more effective than making large ones and is less likely to interrupt your mindfulness.

If you're having pain in your legs, you might want to reconsider which position you're sitting in. Beginners who try to sit in full lotus, for example, just might not have the flexibility to do it. Full lotus can put a lot of pressure on your ankles, knees, or lower back, so maybe you ought to hold off on this one. But if you really want to get into it, try practicing some yoga first to lengthen muscles and tendons and loosen your joints.

If you suffer from a back injury or have knee or joint problems, then it's okay not to sit cross-legged in the iconic meditation position. You can just sit in a chair, if you like. The point is to be relaxed, but not too relaxed. So try not to slouch or lean back too much. If all else fails, lie down on your back with your legs straight and your arms by your side. I personally don't highly recommend this position because you're more likely to fall asleep, but if the pain is pretty bad, it might be your best bet.

One last word on pain in meditation: Sometimes the pain is not such a big deal. It can even be an advantage. It brings your awareness into the body and prevents you from distraction. And one of the goals of meditation is to bring body and mind together so they function as a single unit. So if your posture is okay and the pain is not overwhelming, it might be better for you not to do anything at all, but just sit with it and be mindful of it. That way you can learn to relate to the pain directly and mindfully. There's a lesson to be learned from that. Sometimes the pain just disappears on its own without our having to do anything at all. If this happens to you, then congratulations, you just experienced a lesson in impermanence.

- Sleepiness. I'm sure every meditator experiences this at least once in their career. You're sitting there, trying to be mindful of the breath, but your eyelids just feel so heavy . . . . They just don't want to stay open. Your vision might become cloudy, your mind feels fuzzy and doesn't want to stay on the breath. You begin to drift, and you feel the dark forgetfulness of sleep calling to you. . . .

Sounds like maybe instead of meditating, you need to take a nap. It's crucial, not just for meditation, but also for your health and your success, to make sure you get plenty of rest. Later in this book I will go into more detail about the importance of rest. But if you find yourself nodding off on the cushion, then maybe it's time to go take a power nap.

Alternately, you might consider what time you meditate. If you're doing your practice in the evening after a long, busy day, then you're probably just too tired to meditate at that time. Try doing your session in the morning. Adjust your schedule a bit to make it work, if you need to. If you're only doing one session a day, it's better to do it in the morning, anyway, because you'll be able to bring that meditative awareness with you as you carry on with your day.

If you're already meditating in the morning, but still dozing off when you sit, then you're probably not getting enough sleep at night. Go to bed earlier. Try to get seven or eight hours of sleep. Turn off all the screens at least an hour before bed. The harsh, blue light of computers, televisions, and devices interferes with our sleep patterns by making our brains think it's still daylight.

Likewise, fluorescent lights, including CFLs, have been shown to interfere with sleep patterns, not to mention increase stress hormones. So the fluorescent bulbs have got to go. The best kind of light in the evening, in my experience, comes from incandescent bulbs—if they are still available in your country. If not, you can purchase LED bulbs that give off a softer, yellow light. You might want to look into halogen bulbs, also.

One other thing you can do is have a cup of tea before you meditate. Coffee or yerba mate might work, also—I personally love it—but you might find the dose of caffeine is too strong and makes your mind too active during meditation.

There are many other things that can make you sleepy during meditation, also: meditating after a heavy meal, or when your body is too warm (try taking off extra layers, or turn the heat down or the AC on). Your posture might be off, also. If you're leaning too far back, not keeping your back straight, or slumping your shoulders, it can make you drowsy. So try straightening up and see if that does the trick. If the drowsiness is not overwhelming, there are little remedies and tricks you can try. One is imagining your entire body is filled with a bright, golden light, and that your body becomes lighter and lighter. That might just do the job and wake you up!

- Too many thoughts. Way too many. Like I said before,

thoughts and distractions are not regarded as a problem in meditation. But sometimes they become simply too many, like a great big wall of thoughts. The mind becomes extremely excitable, and you might even feel nervous, irritable, or agitated because of them. In extreme cases, you might even find it hard to sit still.

The best thing you can do is to sit with these restless thoughts and feelings and be mindful of them. Don't try to change them, but just let them exist in their own space. Feel their texture fully. Where does this restlessness register in your body? Can you separate the thoughts that come along with restlessness from the bare physical sensation? Pay attention to the impermanence and shifting nature of the restlessness, also. This will give you insight into its nature.

One thing you can do if this persists and becomes a major problem for you is check and see if you've taken coffee or medicines that might be tweaking you out. For example, if you're in the habit of downing big cups of coffee in the morning before you get on the cushion, then you've found your culprit. Try foregoing that coffee next time or replacing it with a milder stimulant, like green tea. Certain cold medicines, like Sudafed, have the same effect, making you feel jittery and weird. You could try taking a smaller dose.

But it could just be that there are too many things going on in your life, and the stress and anxiety have put your mind into overdrive. Then, when you sit down and stop your activities, suddenly all those thoughts and worries kick in big time.

Meditation definitely helps with the stress and raw nerves, but if you feel overwhelmed whenever you sit down with yourself, you might want to try exercising, taking long walks, getting more rest, getting a massage, listening to soothing music—whatever works to calm yourself down and lower that nervous energy.

If you're having a hard time in your life, you should consider removing the stressors, if you can. Are you in stuck in a toxic relationship, for example? Is your boss a horror? Are you unemployed? Overwhelmed by financial difficulties? Meditation is not a cure for not taking care of these areas of your life, so you'll need to address them head on with the courage and guts we talked about earlier. What meditation can do is help you cultivate more clarity, wisdom, and patience for dealing with life's problems. But we'll go into more detail in a later section on what to do when everything is going wrong.

- Boredom. We talked a little bit about "It sounds boring" as an excuse for not meditating. So now let's talk about what happens when you actually get bored. Just sitting there, doing nothing, you might just want to be anywhere else than where you are right now.

  If you're feeling bored, that means you're onto something. It means you're not entertaining yourself with daydreams and thoughts, or caught up in a hopped-up experience of "meditative" bliss. Because of your practice, all these ways of entertaining yourself have dropped away, and now you feel bored.

  So boredom is a good sign. Just keep sitting with the boredom. You just sit, and sit, and sit. When the session is over and you get back up, it's time to wash the dishes, iron your clothes, or eat breakfast and go to work. It's very boring, and there's no chance of escape. As you settle into this boredom, you will come to appreciate the straightforwardness and lack of self-entertainment. After some time, the experience of boredom becomes very refreshing, honest, and reliable.

- Strange sensations or experiences. During meditation, people sometimes have weird sensations and experiences. There can be distorted feelings in the body, such as body parts feeling like they're expanding or shrinking, or sensations that parts of the body are disappearing. Some see swirling, colored lights moving across their field of vision, hear loud noises, or experience synesthesia or any number of strange visions and sounds.

Sometimes these sensations and experiences may be fascinating; at other times they may be alarming. But in either case, they're really nothing to worry or get excited about. When your concentration becomes deeper and your body stiller, the effect is a kind of sensory deprivation. Your sense organs—eyes, ears, sense of touch, etc.—aren't getting much stimulation, and the brain isn't accustomed to that. So, for example, if there's no stimulation in your field of vision, the visual cortex might become active anyway to fill in the blanks. And that creates the illusion of swirling lights and the like.

Such experiences are signs that your mind is becoming calmer, your mindfulness deeper, and your meditation more and more one-pointed. But they're not anything special, nor are they particularly problematic. So don't worry or feel afraid.

Thi̶ ̶ ̶ ̶ ̶ ̶̶v̶oid in Meditation

e talked about common problems in meditation. These problems are all obviously problems; when they come up, they present themselves as something to be solved. But there are other things you might be doing in your meditation practice that don't seem so obviously problematic at first. Still, they're bad for your practice and best avoided. Here are a few examples:

- Inconsistent practice. I've said it before and I'll say it again: You should strive to keep a consistent practice. If you skip a day for this or that reason, it will be that much easier to skip the next day. The whole continuity of your practice will fall apart, and you'll lose that touch of mindful awareness in everyday life. So keep a daily practice going and don't make excuses for yourself.

- Trying to force it. Meditation is not like other endeavors, where insistence pays off. In mindfulness, if you try to force your concentration, your mind will revolt against you. It will suddenly bolt off in some direction, like an anxious horse with you riding in the saddle. So be gentle with yourself and with your attention. Don't push too hard. But don't be too lackadaisical about it, either. Make an effort, but make a relaxed effort. At first, it may be

41

hard to strike the right balance. But a big part of meditation is learning the right amount of effort to exert so that you remain alert and aware, but avoid tension.

- Impatience for results. Once you've been sitting for awhile, you might start to feel disappointed with meditation and wonder where are the big benefits that were offered? The short answer is that you won't see benefits overnight. It's just like if you start weight training, it's going to take some time before you have a six-pack and tree-trunk biceps. So relax and settle in for the ride. It's a process.

The constant expectancy of results, coming at your practice with an agenda that you want to get this or that, runs counter to the spirit of meditation. Meditation is about relaxing your agenda, just spending some time to get to know yourself. The benefits will not be immediately obvious. But they will start to change your life in subtle ways. Your life might seem to change direction only slightly. But if you keep going in that direction, when you reach the end of the journey, the destination will be completely different from wherever you were headed before.

So sit down, relax, be mindful, and make friends with

yourself. Don't try to make anything happen—just let it happen. That may be hard to do at first, but learning this skill is actually one of the key benefits of meditation.

- Getting attached to experiences. One of the signs of deepening concentration in meditation is that certain kinds of experiences come up. You may have a feeling of tremendous bliss. Or you might have a sense of clarity. You may experience lights or visions or have any number of experiences that feel profound or spiritual to you.

Three words: it's a trap. Sure, such experiences can be signs that your meditation is developing and getting deeper. But they are also incredibly seductive. Once you begin having them, whenever you sit on the cushion, you try to induce them again. You try to work yourself up, work your mind back into the experiences that you crave, because you've become attached to them. When you fail to contrive the same experiences again, you feel disappointed. You think that the quality of your meditation has gone down and you're failing to achieve the same levels as before.

That can be very discouraging and even make you want to give up on meditation altogether. So it's better not to let it get to that point in the first place. If you have some kind of experience in meditation, instead of getting suckered by its seductive quality, just get up off the cushion. End your session right then and there and go walk around a bit, make some tea, relax. Then, the next time you sit, you'll sit without a sense of expectancy that there will be some special experience in store for you.

Mindfulness in Everyday Life

Mindfulness is not just something that takes place on the meditation cushion. Meditation can be seen as the formal practice of mindfulness, or like a mindfulness dress rehearsal. Just as baseball players do spring training to prepare for the real baseball season, meditation is a way of training the mind so that mindfulness is already a well-ingrained habit when we encounter the consequential situations of everyday life.

There is nothing that rules out the application of mindfulness in any situation. Remember Jon Kabat-Zinn's definition of mindfulness from earlier. Mindfulness, he says, is *paying attention on purpose, in the present moment, nonjudgmentally.*

We can pay attention to anything. In fact, we are never *not* paying attention to something. But are we paying attention *on purpose, in the present moment, nonjudgmentally?* The mindfulness you develop on the meditation cushion can reap rich rewards when you bring it into the situations of your life off the cushion.

So, for example, when walking, you can be mindful of the sensation of your feet touching the ground, feeling a sense of your body's weight as the balance shifts from one foot to the other. Is the ground hard or soft? Is the air on your skin warm or cool? Pay attention to the richness of your sensory experience.

You can do the same when eating. Allow yourself to smell the aroma of the food on your plate. Really look at and appreciate the colors of your meal. As you eat, slowly savor each bite, paying close attention to its various flavors. Also give a thought to where your food comes from, all the people and processes involved in growing, harvesting, and transporting your food, and so on. If you eat meat, take a moment to appreciate the life and death of the animal whose flesh now nourishes your body. That is also a kind of mindfulness.

Touch and Go

Sometimes you might be in the middle of a mentally demanding task, and it won't make sense to apply your attention to the fullness of your present-moment sensory experience. In that case, there is a lot of benefit from practicing what Tibetan teacher Chögyam Trungpa called *touch and go*. Whenever you remember to, in the midst of any activity, just take a moment to pay attention to the background, the space, in which your experience is occurring. Allow your mind to rest in that space for just a moment. Then let go of it. Don't try to force your mind to rest there.

I talked a bit earlier about the experience of space in mindfulness. This is a sense that your mind is opening up, that thoughts are lighter or more transparent. It's an awareness, not of all the number of individual events and things going on at any moment, but of the total context or background in which they occur. So with touch-and-go, you take a moment to just let your mind touch on that background or space, and then you let go. Without trying to maintain the sense of space, you just gently return your attention to whatever was engaging it before.

In time, the quality of space will begin to permeate your ordinary experience more and more. You will have a more complete awareness of your thoughts and feelings, of your own mental environment. You will notice things about other people that you had never noticed before. It's like gaining a new intuition into yourself and others. You will become more sensitive to the positive and negative qualities of situations and know when to remove yourself from a toxic environment. The practice of mindfulness makes you quite sensitive and aware of things that would have slipped beneath your radar before.

Take a Calming Walk in Nature

It may sound strange to say this, but mindfulness is not all about the mind. It's also about your body and your environment. The latter are supports for the mind. If you are not taking care of your body's health, if your environment is emotionally toxic or contains too much stimulation, then forget practicing mindfulness and refining your attention. Your mind will not even feel basically healthy or rested.

One of the most pleasant ways of giving gentle exercise to your body while changing your environment is to take a long walk in nature—preferably in the morning or the afternoon, when the sun is low in the sky. The human mind delights in a natural environment. Beautiful, green nature will make you feel relaxed and cause your stress and worry to go down. It eases any kind of depression or anxiety you might have.

You could go on a hike in the woods, near a river, or in a field somewhere, or to a park if you live in a city and it's more convenient. Just walk without any distractions. Don't bring any devices with you—and put your phone on silent and keep it in your pocket the whole time. Leave the headphones at home. Just take in the scenery with all your senses.

You could practice mindful walking, if you like. You could just rest in an open, spacious awareness without any particular focus. Or you could let your mind drift and wander at will. It's up to you. The point is to give the mind some time to relax in a natural environment that's pleasing to you. It really will do you a world of good.

Chapter 2. Mindfulness and the Attitudes of Success

If you're like most people, you probably associate meditation with saffron-clad monks in gentle mountain retreats, far removed from the hustle and bustle of the real world. You may be wondering what, exactly, mindfulness has to do with success. Or maybe, based on what I've already said, you're already starting to get an idea of how mindfulness can be helpful to increase success.

Still, I'm sure we can bring it all into sharper focus and make it very clear just how mindfulness can help you inculcate the qualities of mind you need to be successful in any endeavor. I've already identified several successful qualities of mind that you should work to develop in yourself if you want to achieve success. I talked about *embracing change*, *taking charge of destiny*, *curiosity*, *appreciating interdependence*, and the *courageous spirit*.

How can mindfulness help with developing these qualities? Let's take a look at them one by one.

Embracing Change

Change is a true constant in our world, something the ancients understood very well. Heraclitus, the Greek philosopher known for his theory of flux, famously said that you can never step into the same river twice. And the Buddha, Siddhartha Gautama, also emphasized the transience of things, saying, "All conditioned phenomena are impermanent."

Modern science has deepened our understanding of the constancy of change. The cells in your body have a limited lifespan. Your skin cells, for example, only live for about two or three weeks. And at the quantum level, the energy even in a vacuum is in a state of constant, random fluctuation.

Things are not different at the level of lived experience. Change occurs all the time. Money moves in and out of bank accounts. Jobs are shipped overseas. Spurred by technological innovation, new industries come into being. Your car breaks down. You meet an interesting stranger and spark a deep friendship. The heat of summer gives way to the cold of winter, which again yields to the changing of the seasons.

Some changes are trivial, some deeply consequential; some slow, others sudden and swift; some are predictable, while others are completely unexpected. One of the fruits of mindfulness is that, by refining your attention, you can easily observe the many changes happening at gross and subtle levels around you all the time. With a deeper understanding of impermanence comes that coveted mental trait of successful people, adaptability to change. That is, in other words, the intuitive skill of knowing when to hitch your wagon to new trends so that you are always moving forward and never left in the dust—and it comes with attention to ongoing events and the willingness to accept things as they are.

Taking Charge of Your Destiny

Mindfulness meditation may seem like a passive activity, unsuited to the rough-and-tumble world of modern markets. Sure, you may be thinking, it would be nice to hang out in some mountain hermitage or forest retreat, serene and unfazed by the chaotic events of the world. But how will that help you in your busy life, full of activity, worldly responsibilities, threats, and opportunities?

But mindfulness is not just about relaxation and destressing. It is, as I've emphasized before, about deepening your familiarity with your mind, and making friends with yourself at a fundamental level. Part of this process is accepting your own agency and responsibility for directing the course of your life. A mindful person does not dumbly wait for good luck to fall into their lap—and neither does a successful person. Instead, they actively work to create the causes and conditions for realizing their ambitions. They understand that they, and they alone, shoulder the responsibility of making a success of their life.

One of the strongest motivators for giving up the passive habit is the same understanding of impermanence—that is, the constancy of change—that I was just talking about. Let the fact that time never stops its relentless passage be your inspiration, a reminder that you have no time to waste in achieving your dreams. In other words, the clock's a-ticking, so get moving and seize the day!

Curiosity

Maybe the word "curiosity" does not make the point strongly enough. There should be a sense that the world is a fascinating and exciting place with many kinds of experience and knowledge to offer. Challenges are not just irritating requirements, chores you have to do if you want to get from point A to point B. Instead, you could approach them with a sense of discovery and wonder.

That is the attitude of a successful person. Such people do not consider the responsibilities and challenges of life to be impositions, but instead ride forth to confront chaos with the knowledge that it contains dangers, yes, but is also the source of all treasures. They have the inner disposition of a knight who boldly approaches the dragon with the audacity to steal the gold it hoards.

While we're on the subject of dragons, do you remember Bilbo Baggins from *The Hobbit*? He started off as a timid, boring homebody who wanted absolutely nothing to do with the hazardous world outside his village. He thought he would just sit in his tidy hole in the ground for the rest of his life while the events of the greater world passed him by—and that was just fine by him. But he was forced out the door and onto the open road. The experience transformed him into an adventurer with a sense of wonder and excitement, who had the sheer guts to rob treasure from a very dangerous, very greedy dragon. After that, he could never again be content with a boring life.

To slay a dragon without getting burnt to a crisp, you need to have your wits about you, just like Bilbo Baggins. Your eyes need to be wide open, and you must be attentive to what's going on around you. That, incidentally, is also the practice of mindfulness. Inattentive, incurious courage is just as useless as cowardice—if you want to be successful, that is.

Appreciating Interdependence

Contrary to Simon and Garfunkel, no one is a rock or an island. Actually, that's kind of the point of that song. The narrator is a sad, lonesome person who shuts out human connection because he is afraid of suffering pain and vulnerability.

The fact is, no one is really alone, and no one accomplishes anything by their own efforts only. If you drive to work every day to bust your ass trying to get a promotion, you may think that no one is helping you do that. But the workers who paved the road you drive on are your helpers, and the taxpayers who funded the roadwork are your accomplices. Someone made that car you're driving in. To navigate workplace politics, you first of all need colleagues to compete with. Even your rivals are like a whetstone on which you sharpen the blade of your skills and competence.

I mention this because there is a certain mental attitude that says, *I'm going it alone, I never got any help, so screw you.* But the truth is closer to, *I live and breathe a world of my peers, my friends and enemies. This world is the arena of my action; the people in it will be my helpers and, finally, the witnesses to my success. So it's worthwhile to feel some gratitude to the people in my life and to take care of my relationships with them.*

Mindfulness is not just paying attention to the sensation of the breath, slowly enjoying the taste of food, and that sort of thing. It's also about paying attention to the details of the relationships we have with others and seeing all the different ways that they show us kindness or meanness. It's about paying attention to our own behavior, the way we treat others.

We want other people to treat us well—but do we treat them well? We want fairness—but are we fair with others? To answer this question, we need the courage to be honest with ourselves in case the answer is *no*. It takes guts to apply the mirror of mindfulness to yourself.

To be successful in our goals, we need others. That realization should be both humbling and empowering. If we build our friendships with others with attention and care, we will reap rich dividends in the future. And think about it: even if you became a billionaire by the go-it-alone route, who would you enjoy that wealth with if everyone thought you were a jerk? At best, you'd be surrounded by sycophants and enemies pretending to be your friends, but all scheming against you. A truly successful person is mindful of relationships, cultivating them with the care of a gardener.

The Courageous Spirit

It goes without saying that anything meaningful you want to accomplish in life will require persistence. Persistence, in turn, requires confidence and faith in yourself when the going gets tough and the signals you're getting from your environment and other people all seem to be negative. Basically, no road that you travel will be all clear. All kinds of obstacles, setbacks, and disappointments will occur. In those situations, it is the habit of an *unsuccessful* person to lose heart and give up.

One of the biggest benefits of mindfulness is learning to work with negativity, which I covered in the section on nonjudgmental awareness. It's all too easy to confuse our thoughts with reality, especially if those thoughts have some strong emotional force behind them. When we encounter great difficulty, the emotions behind the thoughts can be very strong and very negative. The thoughts hang over us like a dark cloud, filling us with doubt and confusion. *I'm not smart enough, not talented enough, not courageous enough.... I'll never be a success. I should just give up. How can I compete with all the other people who are so much more competent and qualified than me?*

Experienced meditators can tell you that such thoughts do not just magically disappear when you practice mindfulness. But something quite remarkable happens instead. The way you *relate* to the thoughts changes. Mindfulness opens up space. The more you practice, the more spacious and open your mind becomes. There seems to be no limit to this. The space just keeps expanding. Negative thoughts, self-doubt, and self-criticism become mere echoes. In the same way an echo sounds hollow, negative thoughts seem transparent, fleeting, and lacking substance.

The experience of openness that comes through the practice of mindfulness is incredibly accommodating. It doesn't have to neutralize negative thoughts. It can accommodate negative emotions and doubts. It can accommodate their energy. It can allow them to hang out in the space of the mind until they calm down all on their own. Since you're not gripped by the nagging negative dialogue of your mind, you find that your experience is very fresh and inspiring. You feel inspired to confidence—not any contrived kind of confidence, but basic, natural confidence that comes from not getting knocked off your seat by the mind's gossip. With that natural and easy confidence, you can conquer the many difficulties that will present themselves on your road to success.

Chapter 3. Mindfulness Techniques for Success

Now that we've set the mood by discussing mindfulness, how to establish a practice, and how it all fits together with having the mind of a successful person, let's get to the meat of the matter. I want to offer you some mindfulness techniques that you can use as part of you toolkit on your path to success.

These techniques assume that you've already set the context by maintaining a daily mindfulness practice. Your daily practice, in the morning or evening, will be the anchor that moors your path within an overall atmosphere of expanded awareness and relaxed but focused, alert attention.

The Importance of Rest

The first "technique" is not so much a technique as an important point about how to treat your mind and body if you want to be successful in anything. Many people on the path to success are so driven by their ambitions that they neglect their own mental and physical health. They forget to rest.

Remember, mindfulness is largely about being kind to yourself.

But even if you have a disciplined, daily practice of mindfulness and are diligent in using mindfulness techniques in the pursuit of your goals, all of that will only lead to burnout or a breakdown if you don't take the time to let your mind and body rest. The key thing to understand about rest is that it's important to spend some of your time on things that are not part of your to-do list.

Let's talk about the body first, because resting the body is the precondition for resting the mind. While we could say that resting the mind is a sort of synonym for meditation, resting the body means to give it whatever it needs to feel healthy, relaxed, and comfortable. That includes things like adequate sleep, a good diet, some sunshine and exercise.

This point can be highly individual. For instance, for some people, resting the body might involve getting a massage. Others might prefer taking a swim. But I think we can all agree that, whoever you are, you need enough *sleep*. Specifically, keeping a regular sleep schedule and getting seven to nine hours of sleep a night will ward off fatigue, lack of motivation, moodiness, and stress, among other symptoms of sleep deprivation.

We already touched upon one way to optimize sleep: turning off all the screens at least an hour before going to bed. Cell phones, computers, televisions—the constant flow of information doesn't allow our minds to feel any space and interferes with our sleep patterns. Instead of hooking up your brain to technology in the evening, try reading a book. Take a short, relaxed walk around the neighborhood at night. Spend some time with your partner or spouse, or your dog or cat, if you have one. Skeptical? Prove me wrong. Try disconnecting from all devices for an hour in the evening every day for a week, and see for yourself how you feel afterwards.

Exercise is also an important component of rest. It may not sound very restful, but it's important for your overall physical and mental wellbeing. Yoga is a very restful way of exercising your body that has a number of benefits for both body and mind. But it doesn't have to be yoga. Other relaxing practices, such as tai chi, are also goods ways of boosting your health. If you don't already have an exercise routine, it will be well worth the effort to learn yoga or something like it.

Don't Get Knocked Off Your Seat

When you maintain your seat, it's as if, whatever you do, your basic stance is solid and immovable. You are not a flimsy or frivolous person, because you hold your awareness steadily, with dignity and stability. As long as you keep your seat, obstacles, setbacks, disappointments, negative thoughts, politics, drama—none of them can faze you.

But sometimes something comes along that throws you for a loop. It doesn't have to be bad news, although it often is. It could even be something apparently positive, like the unexpected good luck of winning money or falling in love. Or it could be that some hard work you did finally paid off, and you feel just ecstatic about it. At that time, if you allow sudden events or surprises to make you lose the solidity and stability with which you hold your mind, you have lost your seat.

When that happens, it's important not to let strong positive or negative emotions sweep you up in their current. Neither should you try to repress them with stoic discipline. Instead, practice the gentle method of touch-and-go that we talked about earlier. Touch on the spacious, meditative quality of mindful awareness that you've experienced in your meditation, then just as easily let it go. This reestablishes your presence of mind and brings you back to your seat.

Take a Mindful Break

Whatever you are trying to accomplish, if you want to be successful and change your life, you need focus and sustained effort. But if you become a workaholic, insensitive to your own needs, you will quickly find the *quality* of your focus and effort diminishing. **You can't keep a high cognitive load on your brain all the time.** Sometimes you need to give yourself a chance to stop and catch your breath.

The best way to catch your breath, in my experience, is to practice a few mindful minutes *with* the breath. When you find yourself getting tired and losing focus, don't try to force it. Get up from your desk, if you're at a desk. Go outside or gaze out the window. If the view includes sunlight and trees, all the better. The brain loves natural scenery.

Stop and breathe. Just focus on the breath as you do in your regular mindfulness meditation practice. Breathe out, letting the breath dissolve in the space outside you. Follow the breath with your mind as you inhale again.

Do this for a couple of minutes, then just drop any effort altogether. Don't try to focus on the breath or do anything in particular with your attention. If your mind wants to wander, let it wander. If it wants to settle down, let it settle down. If it wants to think, let it think. If it wants to worry, let it worry. When you take a mindful break, whatever comes up in the mind is okay—just remain mindful of it. Pay attention to what is happening when you let the mind relax and do its own thing.

After a five-minute mindful break, your mind will feel rested and restored. When you get back to work, you'll find that you have more focus and energy and can more easily tackle complicated tasks. I recommend taking a mindful break every one or two hours. You should also take a mindful break any time you begin to feel dull and distracted while working on something.

I'm sure you know the feeling. It's when your eyes glaze over, or you suddenly feel an urge to do anything but what you're doing. **That's a sign that you haven't given your mind a chance to rest, and now it's succumbing to fatigue.** At that time, it's important remember one of the cardinal rules of mindfulness practice: be kind to yourself. I really can't emphasize this point enough. Being kind to yourself involves understanding your needs—body and mind—and providing for them.

With time, and with a mature practice, these needs will be very obvious to you, because you'll be paying attention. That signals that your practice is working—and it's also one of the habits of a successful person.

Be True to Yourself

One of the fruits of mindfulness practice is a decrease in self-deception and a growing awareness of who you are and what are your authentic, core, innermost values. But this awareness can complicate your life if it turns out that the path you're on is in disagreement with your most authentic self.

With increased and more accurate, precise introspection, you will come to understand many things about yourself. Don't resist this new understanding. Cultivate it. Actively look at your mind and develop a sense of curiosity about yourself. **Get to know yourself, what you really value and believe deep down.** Don't be afraid to do some deep sea diving into your own mind.

If you do find that the way you live your life, or your occupation and livelihood are inconsistent with your authentic, inmost values and beliefs, then you yourself must take the responsibility for changing your life. **After all, success in something that disagrees with you fundamentally is not any kind of success worth having.**

Notice New Things

Let's again go back to Kabat-Zinn's useful definition of mindfulness from before. Mindfulness is "paying attention on purpose...." In this technique, we use our attention to always keep an eye out for new things, new trends, new ideas. We try to work new solutions and ways of doing things into our lives as a way of keeping things fresh. The upside is that we raise our energy level and discover better ways of doing things.

Mindfulness ought to make you alert, so that you're more aware of your surroundings and more readily notice things in your environment. This is, again, just paying attention on purpose. Say you're in sales. What are some of the sales techniques your colleagues are using? Are they working well, or not? Pay attention to these sorts of things and you'll learn a lot.

You can work new ideas gleaned from your observations into your own methods. You can even take an experimental approach and come up with entirely new ideas of your own. There's no limit to this. One of the advantages of this technique is that this exploratory, experimental method will increase your curiosity about the world and impart a sense of freshness and excitement to what you do. But the biggest benefit, of course, is that you will discover new and better ways of achieving your goals.

"One Bird, One Stone"

One of the most foolish notions we've had drilled into our heads in our hectic modern age is the idea of multitasking. If you're like me, you've been exposed again and again to the idea that the ability to multitask is a hallmark of a successful and productive person, that in order to accomplish many things in the shortest timeframe, you need to do many things at once.

Well, that's wrong. Multitasking is something computers do. But we are not computers. We're human beings, and our minds don't work like that. Maybe you've seen a demotivational poster to the effect that multitasking is "the art of doing twice as much as you should half as well as you could." It turns out that's true.

The problem is that the mind only pays attention to one thing at a time. There is no such thing as paying attention to two or even three things at a time. What actually happens when you try to do this is that your attention switches back and forth between two or more different tasks. It's kind of like trying to juggle three balls—if you only had one hand. The cognitive load demanded by switching your attention again and again expends energy. But that energy could be better used on doing *one* thing and doing it well.

Don't just take my word for it. The mental wastefulness of multitasking is now well established by psychological research. Researchers at Stanford University found that multitaskers had worse attention spans and worse memories than subjects who focused on one task at a time. They found that the multitaskers were, surprisingly, even worse at switching between tasks. Single taskers were able to switch to new tasks faster than multitaskers.[8] You heard that right: multitaskers are not even good at *multitasking!* To me, that sounds pretty mindless, not mindful.

So don't try to hit two birds with one stone. Hit one bird with one stone. Do one thing at a time, and do it mindfully—and you'll find your productivity increasing.

Let Go of Drama

Conflict is pretty much unavoidable. Even if you try to avoid it, it will somehow find you out in the end. That goes for the workplace as well as anywhere else.

But do you think successful people let their minds get so entangled in workplace politics and personal conflict that they

---

8   Ophir, Eyal et al., "Cognitive control in media multitaskers," *Proceedings of the National Academy of Sciences* 106 no 37 (2009) , 15583–15587.

allow the drama to take them on a detour that costs precious time and emotional resources? No, I don't think so either. If you spend your time resenting the conflicts you have with someone else, chances are that person will move on and you'll be left stuck in the same place, obsessing about old news.

My advice is: Don't let anyone step all over you, but don't hang on to resentment, either. With the practice of mindfulness, you will learn to allow space for your emotions to settle down. Resentment will naturally fade away on its own if your mind is relaxed.

So if you find yourself stuck in a loop, thinking again and again about some personal drama, take a mindful break. Don't try to force your mind away from its feelings, or repress any lingering emotions. Allow them to exist as they are—but don't let them hook you, either.

Particularly helpful for letting go of bad blood is to try to consider matters from a different perspective. Mindfulness breeds an attitude of self-honesty, which is the courage to look at yourself without the usual stories in which you play the hero or the victim. With this attitude, hold a mirror to yourself and ask yourself: Are you really completely innocent, or do you share at least some of the blame?

Also try considering things from the other person's perspective. Whatever they did, how did it make sense to do it from their perspective, in their situation? Put yourself in their shoes, think about the context of their actions, and maybe it will all seem more understandable to you. Forgiveness is a virtue that will benefit you more than anyone else.

Don't get stuck on hurt feelings or hurt pride. That way lies failure and bitterness. Instead, with an attitude of kindness to yourself and others, shake it off and continue on your merry way.

Forgive Your Mistakes

You've probably heard again and again that everybody makes mistakes, and you should learn from your mistakes, etc. We hear these things so many times they become just clichés, mere noise in the echo chamber. But maybe we're not so sure how to learn from our mistakes, because we're so busy feeling bad about them. Nothing will derail our road to achievement and success like a guilty conscience or a mind full of regrets.

The spacious quality of emotional objectivity and critical distance cultivated in mindfulness meditation comes into play here. If we see our own mistakes against their natural background, it takes some of the sting out of the guilt or regret that we feel. Mindfulness trains the mind to relate to negativity in a healthier way, so that we don't stew in bad feelings and self-criticism as if we couldn't stop picking at a scab.

Instead of practicing regret, instead of practicing beating yourself up, try practicing self-forgiveness. It's okay to make mistakes. Just try not to make the same mistake twice. Instead, consider carefully what you need to change about yourself or your ways of doing things to keep the same mistake from happening again.

Chapter 4. When Everything Goes Wrong

Sometimes life knocks us in the dust and doesn't give us a hand back up. Sudden events or tragedies, such as a death in the family, colossal disappointments, huge losses—so many things can cause the ground to just disappear from under our feet and leave us just falling through the air.

At such times, forget the usual kinds of negative emotions. We go into absolute turmoil. Or we become completely numb and unfeeling, like zombies, as our mind puts out emotional anesthetic. We feel a total loss of security. We are left without hope, a bundle of frayed nerves, stumbling through our own personal catastrophes.

I've painted a bleak picture, but maybe you're already familiar with it. The fact is, we don't know where or when disaster will hit us. Remember how we talked earlier about not getting knocked off your seat? Hard times will almost certainly knock you off your seat, again and again, and meditation will not take away your pain. But it's important to keep regaining your seat anyway. And it's important to keep up your practice. No, mindfulness won't fix everything. But it will bring you in touch with your center, your innate wisdom. It will allow you to weather your trials with courage and presence of mind.

It's too cute to say it's all a lesson or a test. Whatever is happening in your life, good or bad, is not a rehearsal. It's the real thing. It's your life, and it's happening to you right now. Mindfulness gives you the ability to live it fully, with dignity and grace. Meditation in hard times is about the willingness to expose yourself to life, to make yourself vulnerable again and again, without the fear that it will destroy you—because it won't. Whatever experience you have, no matter how good or bad, will be followed by another experience, and another, and so on. The great meditation teacher Chögyam Trungpa famously said, "The bad news is you're falling through the air, nothing to hang on to, no parachute. The good news is there's no ground."

Whatever we go through in life is all experience. Whether we like it or not, we're always moving forward and things never remain the same. We are always at the edge between the past and the future. And, for all our planning and hedging, the future is a complete unknown, an abyss. We're in no-man's-land, heading into uncertain territory. Meditation is about not running from this reality but having the courage to take whatever comes and willingly confronting the unknown again and again. It is about going forth and finding the challenge rather than waiting for it to come to us.

Three Fierce Mantras

The so-called "three fierce mantras" are mottoes attributed to a 12th-century Tibetan master. They express, very concisely, an undaunted spirit willing to face any challenge or hardship. Repeating them to yourself may give you some courage in trying times. They are:

Whatever is coming, come!

However it goes, so be it!

Nothing whatsoever is necessary.

These three mantras have a gritty determination to them. They show a willingness to accept any and all experience unconditionally. Even if you don't feel like you have the same level of determination, you can still repeat them to yourself whenever you need a quick dose of bravery or a reminder to bring a fearless spirit into your life.

Don't Lose Your Practice

When you're going through hell, it might not always seem relevant to keep up a meditation practice. But hard times are when you need meditation the most. You can't help being shaky at such times. You can't help that life is putting you through the ringer, that you're sometimes falling apart, that you just can't keep it together. In trying times, you could give up and just let life kick you in the rear. You could actually just let yourself go completely, stop caring, stop trying, just let everything fall apart. You absolutely could lie down and surrender to your fear and despair. But I wouldn't recommend it.

Even if everything is going wrong, you can still keep returning to the cushion every day and showing kindness to yourself. You can keep expressing your willingness to work with your mind by sitting and meditating. You can keep up this dignified and noble activity, which allows you to get in touch with that most dignified and noble part of yourself.

What to Do

Those are encouraging words, but let's take a look at some actual concrete steps you can take to cope with difficult times. Like I already said, the first thing you can do is maintain your daily practice. Let it be a rock of stability in your life, a place you can return to when you need to recover your equilibrium. Meditation sustains us, and we need that when times are hard. In addition to that, here we'll present a couple of mindfulness techniques you can use when you're in the thick of it.

R.A.I.N.

Meditation teacher Tara Brach recommends a mindfulness technique called R.A.I.N. for dealing with difficult emotions and difficult times. R.A.I.N. is an acronym for a four-step mindfulness process that cuts through powerful emotions and helps us find our center and equanimity. It stands for:

- Recognize what is happening.
- Allow life to be just as it is.
- Investigate inner experience with kindness.
- Non-identification.

1. Recognize what is happening.

When you're going through difficulty and emotional turmoil, remember to take stock of the moment. Turn your attention to what's happening to you emotionally and recognize it. Ask yourself, "What is happening inside right now?" In other words, check your inner weather and see how it looks. If there's a storm, start with the simple recognition that it's stormy. So the first step is to turn the attention inward and pay attention to what's going on with you emotionally.

2. Allow life to be just as it is.

Whatever you discover inside, whatever emotion is happening, you allow it. Just let it be, let it exist in its own space. You'll probably feel a strong aversion to your emotions at this time, and you might want to suppress the emotions, to resist, change, or fix them in some way. Don't do that. It's important that you allow them to be.

It might help to kind of speak to yourself mentally, to tell yourself something like, "Yes," or "I accept this." Putting a verbal stamp on it strengthens your resolve to accept whatever comes.

When you accept your emotions, you're accepting reality. At this moment you feel desperate, crushed, or whatever feeling you're feeling, but you accept this reality and don't try to change it. You simply give up the struggle against the reality of what's happening in your heart and mind.

3. Investigate inner experience with kindness.

After the first two steps, you may already have reconnected with the presence of awareness and a sense of openness. You might feel no further need to continue. But if recognition and acceptance are not enough, then you can also investigate what's happening in your mind. This is a more specific inquiry into the nature of what you're feeling. Why do I feel this way? Where does this feeling register in my body? What beliefs underlie this emotion? What is this emotion trying to tell me?

You don't need to conduct the questions with any kind of aggression to yourself or your emotions. Make your investigation with kindness, gentleness, and a willingness to accept and forgive yourself. With an attitude of kindness to yourself, this investigation will allow healing to occur and reveal avenues of action to you.

4. Non-Identification

The openness and acceptance of the first three steps lead naturally to the third step, non-identification. Non-identification means that your sense of self is not caught up in the emotions that are happening in your mind. You don't identify with the emotions or tell yourself stories about them. Those emotions are not you and you are not those emotions. Instead, identify with the continuous presence of awareness that witnesses everything within the context of space, which underlies all experience. Identify with the still, spacious center within. You can't force this last step, but if the first three steps went well, they will naturally lead to this sense of expansive, peaceful awareness.

Self-Soothing

Phillip Moffitt of Spirit Rock Meditation Center has a technique for dealing with difficulty which he calls "self-soothing." The idea is that, when we do get knocked off our seat, we lose the equanimity and wisdom of mindfulness, and instead get caught up in reactive patterns. So then we're not dealing with whatever situation we're in in a conscious, deliberate way, but we're getting caught up in all sorts of unconscious, habitual mechanisms. Self-soothing is a way to use mindfulness to regain our balance when we've been thrown off by strong emotions and events. Then we restore the conscious, mindful presence that allows us to handle situations skillfully and creatively. He describes three phases to the self-soothing technique.

1. Re-establish your equilibrium.

First, you calm yourself down using whatever method you prefer. It can be mindfulness of the breath or one of the exercises we mentioned above: mindfulness of sounds, for instance. You can also use the touch-and-go technique. If you've been practicing mindfulness for a while, you might have a go-to method in mind already. Whatever works best for you, use it to find a sense of calm.

Then you identify what's going on inside you. You look within yourself and identify the emotion you're feeling. The person who's doing the looking is the witness to your emotions, you yourself. Look at your emotion with kindness. With compassion for yourself, give yourself comfort and love.

2. Remember your intentions.

Now that you're recovering your balance, remind yourself of your intentions and your commitment to your purposes in life, as well as to the practice of mindfulness. You may not quite know how to get a handle on the situation and proceed just yet, but you've calmed down somewhat, and you've recalled who you are, what you stand for, and what you were doing. You remember what it is you're trying to accomplish in the first place, rather than just freaking out because something happened. This is about making contact with a sense of clarity about yourself. It's very important because the turbulence of situations can make us forget our goals, which causes us to react in ways that undermine us.

3. Redirect your attention.

Now that you've calmed down and remembered what your purpose and intentions are, direct your attention to what insights you can apply to the current situation. Recall the changeable nature of everything, and remind yourself that these hard times, too, will pass. Remind yourself that it's not your fault you're going through difficulties now. Everything happens due to its own set of factors, and this is no exception. There are many variables at play in what's happening in your life right now, and this is just part of the difficulty of life. Take some comfort in knowing that there's nothing extraordinary or unique about having a hard time.

Conclusion

This book is all about deepening your awareness, getting to know yourself, and developing attitudes and mental habits that will make you not only a successful and effective person in life, but a happy and wise one, as well. To that end, I've discussed the general concepts around success and mindfulness, how they relate to each other, and a number of techniques and pointers that can help you along the way.

It bears repeating that the main technique in this book that will make all the other techniques workable is the sitting practice of meditation. Meditation is like the hub of a wheel, and the auxiliary techniques are like the spokes. With all of them working together, you'll have a good, solid wheel capable of taking you from here to there—wherever you want to go.

But the wheel has to rest on solid ground, and even with a perfect wheel, there needs to be some force to turn it. The difference between success and failure is your own effort. The techniques in this book cannot be applied mechanically, because this is not a cookbook or an instruction manual. It is, instead, sort of an introduction to your mind. I mean the kind of introduction that says, "I'd like you to meet someone...."

My hope for you is that you will meet yourself—your true self—on the road, and that this meeting will result in success in achieving your authentic vision for your life. To do this will require patience, courage, carefulness, and hard work—but the payoff is enormous. The payoff is nothing less than transforming your life into its true potential.

In the end, it all depends on you. You alone have to work with yourself and with your mind. Working with yourself is the only way.

The. Only. Way.

And it *is* work. In fact, it's *the* work. It's the most important and worthwhile work you could ever do. So don't delay. Get started *now*. After all, it's your life.

Good luck!

<u>One last thing before you go – Can I ask you a favor? I need your help!</u> If you like this book, could you please share your experience on Amazon and write an honest review? It will be just one minute for you (I will be happy even with one sentence!), but a GREAT help for me and definitely a good Karma ☺. Since I'm not a well-established author and I don't have powerful people and big publishing companies supporting me, <u>I read every single review and jump around with joy like a little kid every time my readers comment on my books and give me their honest feedback!</u> If I was able to inspire you in any way, please let me know! It will also help me get my books in front of more people looking for new ideas and useful knowledge.

If you did not enjoy the book or had a problem with it, please don't   hesitate   to   contact   me at contact@mindfulnessforsuccess.com **and tell me how I can improve it to provide more value and more knowledge to my readers.** I'm constantly working on my books to make them better and more helpful.

Thank you and good luck! I believe in you and I wish you all the best on your new journey!

Your friend,

Ian

My Free Gift to You – <u>Get One of My Audiobooks For Free!</u>

If you've never created an account on Audible (the biggest audiobook store in the world), **you can claim one free audiobook of mine**!
It's a simple process:
1. Pick one of my audiobooks on Audible:
http://www.audible.com/search?advsearchKeywords=Ian+Tuhovsky
Shortened link:
http://tinyurl.com/IanTuhovskyAudiobooks
2. Once you choose a book and open its detail page, click the orange button "Free with 30-Day Trial Membership."
3. Follow the instructions to create your account and download your first free audiobook.
Note that you are NOT obligated to continue after your free

trial expires. You can cancel your free trial easily anytime, and you won't be charged at all.

Also, if you haven't downloaded your free book already:

<u>Discover How to Get Rid of Stress & Anxiety and Reach Inner Peace in 20 Days or Less!</u>

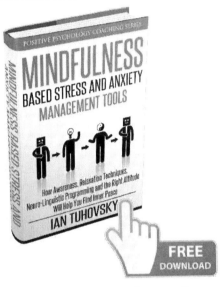

To help speed up your personal transformation, I have prepared a special gift for you!

Download my full, 120 page e-book "Mindfulness Based Stress and Anxiety Management Tools" for free <u>by clicking here.</u>

Link:

<u>tinyurl.com/mindfulnessgift</u>

<u>Hey there like-minded friends, let's get connected!</u>

Don't hesitate to visit:
-My Blog: www.mindfulnessforsuccess.com
-My Facebook fanpage: https://www.facebook.com/mindfulnessforsuccess
-My Instagram profile: https://instagram.com/mindfulnessforsuccess
-My Amazon profile: amazon.com/author/iantuhovsky

Recommended Reading for You:

If you are interested in Self-Development, NLP, Psychology, Social Dynamics, PR, Soft Skills and related topics, you might be interested in previewing or downloading my other books:

<u>Emotional Intelligence Training: A Practical Guide to Making Friends with Your Emotions and Raising Your EQ</u>

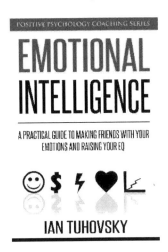

Do you believe your life would be healthier, happier and even better, if you had more practical strategies to regulate your own emotions?

Most people agree with that.
Or, more importantly:
Do you believe you'd be healthier and happier if everyone who you live with had the strategies to regulate their emotions?

...Right?

The truth is not too many people actually realize what EQ is really all about and what causes its popularity to grow constantly.

Scientific research conducted by many American and European universities prove that the **"common" intelligence responses account for less than 20% of our life achievements and successes, while the other over 80% depends on emotional intelligence.** To put it roughly: **either you are emotionally intelligent, or you're doomed to mediocrity, at best.**

As opposed to the popular image, emotionally intelligent people are not the ones who react impulsively and spontaneously, or who act lively and fiery in all types of social environments.

Emotionally intelligent people are open to new experiences, can show feelings adequate to the situation, either good or bad, and find it easy to socialize with other people and establish new contacts. They handle stress well, say "no" easily, realistically assess the achievements of themselves or others and are not afraid of constructive criticism and taking calculated risks. **They are the people of success.** Unfortunately, this perfect model of an emotionally intelligent person is extremely rare in our modern times.

Sadly, nowadays, **the amount of emotional problems in the world is increasing at an alarming rate.** We are getting richer, but less and less happy. Depression, suicide, relationship breakdowns, loneliness of choice, fear of closeness, addictions—this is clear evidence that we are getting increasingly worse when it comes to dealing with our emotions. **Emotional intelligence is a SKILL, and can be learned through constant practice and training, just like riding a bike or swimming!**

This book is stuffed with lots of effective exercises, helpful info and practical ideas.

Every chapter covers different areas of emotional intelligence and shows you, **step by step**, what exactly you can do to **develop your EQ** and become the **better version of yourself**.

I will show you how freeing yourself from the domination of left-sided brain thinking can contribute to your inner transformation—**the emotional revolution that will help you redefine who you are and what you really want from life!**

In This Book I'll Show You:

• What Is Emotional Intelligence and What Does EQ Consist of?
• How to **Observe and Express** Your Emotions
• How to **Release Negative Emotions** and **Empower the Positive Ones**
• How to Deal with Your **Internal Dialogues**
• How to **Deal with the Past**
• **How to Forgive** Yourself and How to Forgive Others
• How to Free Yourself from **Other People's Opinions and Judgments**
• What Are "Submodalities" and How Exactly You Can Use Them to **Empower Yourself** and **Get Rid of Stress**
• The Nine Things You Need to **Stop Doing to Yourself**
• How to Examine Your Thoughts
• **Internal Conflicts** Troubleshooting Technique
• The Lost Art of Asking Yourself the Right Questions and **Discovering Your True Self!**
• How to Create Rich Visualizations
• LOTS of practical exercises from the mighty arsenal of psychology, family therapy, NLP etc.
• **And many, many more!**

Direct Buy Link to Amazon Kindle Store:
https://tinyurl.com/IanEQTrainingKindle
Paperback version on Createspace:
https://tinyurl.com/ianEQpaperback

Communication Skills Training: A Practical Guide to Improving Your Social Intelligence, Presentation, Persuasion and Public Speaking

Do You Know How To Communicate With People Effectively, Avoid Conflicts and Get What You Want From Life?

...It's not only about what you say, but also about WHEN, WHY and HOW you say it.

Do The Things You Usually Say Help You, Or Maybe Hold You Back?

Have you ever considered **how many times you intuitively felt that maybe you lost something important or crucial, simply because you unwittingly said or did something, which put somebody off?** Maybe it was a misfortunate word, bad formulation, inappropriate joke, forgotten name, huge misinterpretation, awkward conversation or a strange tone of your voice?

Maybe you assumed that you knew exactly what a particular concept meant for another person and you stopped asking questions?

Maybe you could not listen carefully or could not stay silent for a moment? **How many times have you wanted to achieve something, negotiate better terms, or ask for** a promotion and failed miserably?

It's time to put that to an end with the help of this book.

<u>**Lack of communication skills is exactly what ruins most peoples' lives.**</u>

If you don't know how to communicate properly, you are going to have problems both in your intimate and family relationships.

You are going to be ineffective in work and business situations. It's going to be troublesome managing employees or getting what you want from your boss or your clients on a daily basis. Overall, **effective communication is like an engine oil which makes your life run smoothly, getting you wherever you want to be.** There are very few areas in life in which you can succeed in the long run without this crucial skill.
What Will You Learn With This Book?

-What Are The **Most Common Communication Obstacles** Between People And How To Avoid Them
-How To Express Anger And Avoid Conflicts
-What Are **The Most 8 Important Questions You Should Ask Yourself** If You Want To Be An Effective Communicator?
-**5 Most Basic and Crucial** Conversational Fixes
-How To Deal With Difficult and Toxic People
-Phrases to **Purge from Your Dictionary** (And What to Substitute Them With)
-The Subtle Art of **Giving and Receiving Feedback**
-Rapport, the **Art of Excellent Communication**
-How to Use Metaphors to **Communicate Better** And **Connect With People**
-What Metaprograms and Meta Models Are and How Exactly To Make Use of Them To **Become A Polished Communicator**
-How To Read Faces and **How to Effectively Predict Future Behaviors**

-How to Finally Start **Remembering Names**
-How to Have a Great Public Presentation
-How To Create Your Own **Unique Personality** in Business (and Everyday Life)
-Effective Networking

Direct link to Amazon Kindle Store:

https://tinyurl.com/IanCommSkillsKindle

Paperback version on Createspace:

http://tinyurl.com/iancommunicationpaperback

Natural Confidence Training: How to Develop Healthy Self-Esteem and Deep Self-Confidence to Be Successful and Become True Friends with Yourself

Positive Psychology Coaching Series

NATURAL
CONFIDENCE
TRAINING:

HOW TO DEVELOP
HEALTHY SELF-ESTEEM
AND
DEEP SELF-CONFIDENCE
TO BE
SUCCESSFUL
AND BECOME
TRUE FRIENDS
WITH YOURSELF

IAN TUHOVSKY

Lack of self-confidence and problems with unhealthy self-esteem are usually the reason why smart, competent and talented people never achieve a satisfying life, a life that should easily be possible for them.

Think about your childhood.
At the age of four or five, there weren't too many

things that you considered impossible, right?
You weren't bothered or held back by any kind of criticism; you stayed indifferent to what other people thought of you. An ugly stain on your sweater, or even worse, on your leggings, was not considered a problem or an obstacle.

You could run on a crowded beach absolutely nude, laughing, go swimming in a city fountain and then play in the sandbox with strawberry ice cream smeared in your hair. Nothing and no one could stop you from saying what you wanted to say, even the silliest things. **There was no shame in your early childhood;** you loved yourself and everyone else.

Can you remember it?
What happened to us?

Parents, teachers, preachers and media **stuffed certain beliefs into your head**, day after day for many years. These beliefs and attitudes **robbed you of your natural, inborn confidence.**
Maybe it was one traumatic experience of some kind that changed you, or maybe it was a slow process that lasted for years. One thing is certain—lacking confidence is not your natural, default state. **It brings you down and now you have to unlearn it.**

Can you name even a single situation in life where high confidence isn't useful?
... Right?

Confidence is not useful only in everyday life and casual situations. Do you really want to fulfill your dreams, or do you just want to keep chatting about them with your friends, until one day you wake up as a grumpy, old, frustrated person?

Big achievements require brave and fearless actions. If you want to act bravely, you need to be confident.
Along with lots of useful, practical exercises, this book will provide you with plenty of new information that will help you

understand what confidence problems really come down to. And this is the most important and the saddest part, because most people do not truly recognize the root problem, and that's why they get poor results.

In this book you will read about:
-How, when and why society robs us all of natural confidence and healthy self-esteem.
-What kind of social and psychological traps you need to avoid to feel much calmer, happier and more confident.
-What "natural confidence" means and how it becomes natural.
-What "self-confidence" really is and what it definitely isn't (as opposed to what most people think!).
-How your mind hurts you when it really just wants to help you, and how to stop the process.
-What different kinds of fear we feel, where they come from and how to defeat them.
-How to have a great relationship with yourself.
-What beliefs and habits you should have and cultivate to succeed.
-How to use stress to boost your inner strength.
-Effective and ineffective ways of building healthy self-esteem.
-How mindfulness and meditation help boost, cultivate and maintain your natural confidence.
-Why the relation between self-acceptance and stress is so crucial.
-How to stay confident in professional situations.
-How to protect your self-esteem when life brings you down and how to deal with criticism and jealousy.
-How to use neuro-linguistic programming, imagination, visualizations, diary entries and your five senses to re-program your subconscious and get rid of "mental viruses" and detrimental beliefs that actively destroy your natural confidence and healthy self-esteem.

In the last part of the book you will find 15 of the most effective, proven and field-tested strategies and exercises that help people transform their lives.

Take the right action and start changing your life for the better today!

Direct Buy Link to Amazon Kindle Store:
https://tinyurl.com/IanConfidenceTraining
https://tinyurl.com/IanConfidencePaperback

Meditation for Beginners: How to Meditate (as an Ordinary Person!) to Relieve Stress and Be Successful

Meditation doesn't have to be about crystals, hypnotic folk music and incense sticks!

Forget about sitting in unnatural and uncomfortable positions while going, "Ommmmm...." It is not necessarily a club full of yoga masters, Shaolin monks, hippies and new-agers.

It is a super useful and universal practice which can improve your overall brain performance and happiness. When meditating, you take a step back from actively thinking your thoughts, and instead see them for what they are. The reason why meditation is helpful in reducing stress and attaining peace is that it gives your over-active consciousness a break.

Just like your body needs it, your mind does too!

I give you the gift of peace that I was able to attain through present moment awareness.

Direct Buy Link to Amazon Kindle Store:

https://tinyurl.com/IanMeditationGuide

Paperback version on Createspace:

http://tinyurl.com/ianmeditationpaperback

Zen: Beginner's Guide: Happy, Peaceful and Focused Lifestyle for Everyone

Contrary to popular belief, Zen is not a discipline reserved for monks practicing Kung Fu. Although there is some truth to this idea, Zen is a practice that is applicable, useful and pragmatic for anyone to study regardless of what religion you follow (or don't follow).

Zen is the practice of studying your subconscious and **seeing your true nature.**

The purpose of this work is to show you how to apply and utilize the teachings and essence of Zen in everyday life in the Western society. I'm not really an "absolute truth seeker" unworldly type of person—I just believe in practical plans and blueprints that actually help in living a better life. Of course I will tell you about the origin of Zen and the traditional ways of practicing it, but I will also show you my side of things, my personal point of view and translation of many Zen truths into a more "contemporary" and practical language.

It is a "modern Zen lifestyle" type of book.

What You Will Read About:
• Where Did Zen Come from? - A short history and explanation of Zen
• What Does Zen Teach? - The major teachings and precepts of Zen
• Various Zen meditation techniques that are applicable and practical for everyone!

- The Benefits of a Zen Lifestyle
- What Zen Buddhism is NOT?
- How to Slow Down and Start Enjoying Your Life
- How to Accept Everything and Lose Nothing
- Why Being Alone Can Be Beneficial
- Why Pleasure Is NOT Happiness
- Six Ways to Practically Let Go
- How to De-clutter Your Life and Live Simply
- "Mindfulness on Steroids"
- How to Take Care of Your Awareness and Focus
- Where to Start and How to Practice Zen as a Regular Person
- And many other interesting concepts...

I invite you to take this journey into the peaceful world of Zen Buddhism with me today!

Direct Buy Link to Amazon Kindle Store:

https://tinyurl.com/IanZenGuide

Paperback version on Createspace:

http://tinyurl.com/ianzenpaperback

Buddhism: Beginner's Guide: Bring Peace and Happiness to Your Everyday Life

Buddhism is one of the most practical and simple belief systems on this planet, and it has greatly helped me on my way to become a better person in every aspect possible. In this book I will show you what happened and how it was.

No matter if you are totally green when it comes to Buddha's teachings or maybe you have already heard something about them—this book will help you systematize your knowledge and will inspire you to learn more and to take steps to make your life positively better!

I invite you to take this beautiful journey into the graceful and meaningful world of Buddhism with me today!

Direct link to Amazon Kindle Store:

https://tinyurl.com/IanBuddhismGuide

Paperback version on Createspace:

http://tinyurl.com/ianbuddhismpaperback

Author's Blog: www.mindfulnessforsuccess.com

Amazon Author Page:

http://www.amazon.com/author/iantuhovsky/

Hi! I'm Ian...

. . . and I am interested in life. I am in the study of having an awesome and passionate life, which I believe is within the reach of practically everyone. I'm not a mentor or a guru. I'm just a guy who always knew there was more than we are told. I managed to turn my life around from way below my expectations to a really satisfying one, and now I want to share this fascinating journey with you so that you can do it, too.

I was born and raised somewhere in Eastern Europe, where Polar Bears eat people on the streets, we munch on snow instead of ice cream and there's only vodka instead of tap water, but since I make a living out of several different businesses, I move to a new country every couple of months. I also work as an HR consultant for various European companies.

I love self-development, traveling, recording music and providing value by helping others. I passionately read and write about social psychology, sociology, NLP, meditation, mindfulness, eastern philosophy, emotional intelligence, time management, communication skills and all of the topics related to conscious self-development and being the most awesome version of yourself.

Breathe. Relax. Feel that you're alive and smile. And never hesitate to contact me!

Made in the USA
San Bernardino, CA
20 January 2018